Classical Sheet Music For Flute With Flute & Piano Duets Book 2

Michael Shaw

Music Arrangements. All music arrangements in this book by **Michael Shaw** **Copyright © 2015**

ISBN: 1517675596
ISBN-13: 978-1517675592

www.mikesmusicroom.co.uk

Contents

Introduction

The sheet music in this book has been arranged for Flute. There are two versions of every piece in this book. The first version is a Flute only arrangement, the second version is a Flute and piano accompaniment arrangement. Skill level for this book is a little more advanced than book 1 and varies from Grade 2 to Grade 4 depending on which piece you are playing. The piano parts in this book can be played on a piano, keyboard or organ.

As well as playing duets with piano in this book you can also play together in a duet or ensemble with other instruments with a classical sheet music book for that instrument. All arrangements are the same and keys are adjusted for B flat, E flat, F and C instruments so everything sounds correct. Piano parts for all instrument books are in the same key.

To get a book for your instrument choose from the *Classical Sheet Music Book 2 with Piano Duets* series. Instruments in this series include, Clarinet, Tenor Saxophone, Alto Saxophone, Oboe, Trumpet, French Horn and Trombone.

Check out my author page to view these books.

Author Page US
 amazon.com/Michael-Shaw/e/B00FNVFJGQ/

Author Page UK
 amazon.co.uk/Michael-Shaw/e/B00FNVFJGQ/

Fur Elise

Flute

Beethoven

1

Fur Elise
Flute & Piano

Beethoven

Theme From Jupiter

Flute

Gustav Holst

Theme From Jupiter

Flute & Piano

Gustav Holst

Radetzky March

Flute

Johann Strauss

Radetzky March

Flute & Piano

Johann Strauss

La Donna E Mobile

Flute

Giuseppe Verdi

La Donna E Mobile

Flute & Piano

Giuseppe Verdi

Valse Lente

Flute

Leo Delibes

Flute

6

Fl.

11

Fl.

16

Fl.

21

Fl.

26

Fl.

30

Fl.

Valse Lente
Flute & Piano

Leo Delibes

Eine Kleine Nachtmusik

Flute

Mozart

Flute

Fl.

Fl.

Fl.

Fl.

Fl.

Fl.

Eine Kleine Nachtmusik

Flute & Piano

Mozart

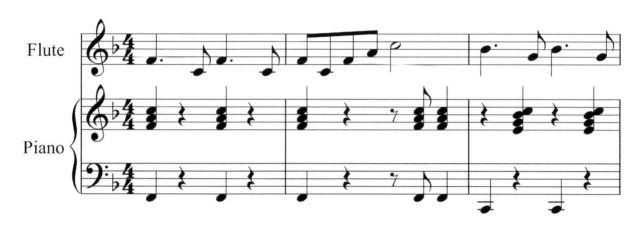

Etude
Flute

Chopin

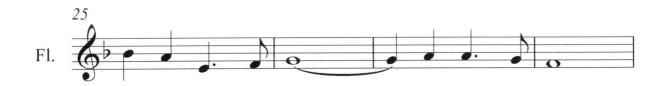

poco rit.

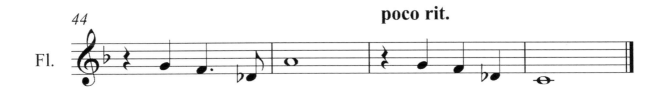

Etude
Flute & Piano

Chopin

26

Liebestraum

Flute

Franz Liszt

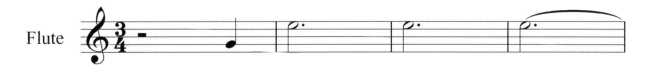

Liebestraum

Flute & Piano

Franz Liszt

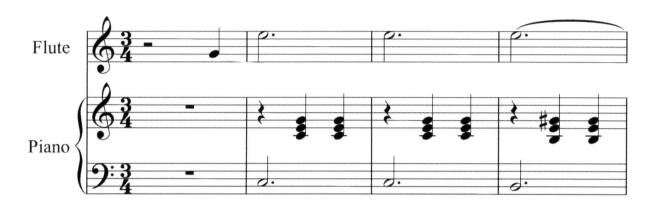

Wedding March

Flute

Richard Wagner

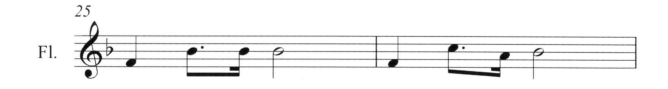

Wedding March

Flute & Piano

Richard Wagner

Sonata In C Major

Flute

Mozart

Flute

Fl.

Fl.

Fl.

Fl.

Fl.

Sonata In C Major

Flute & Piano

Mozart

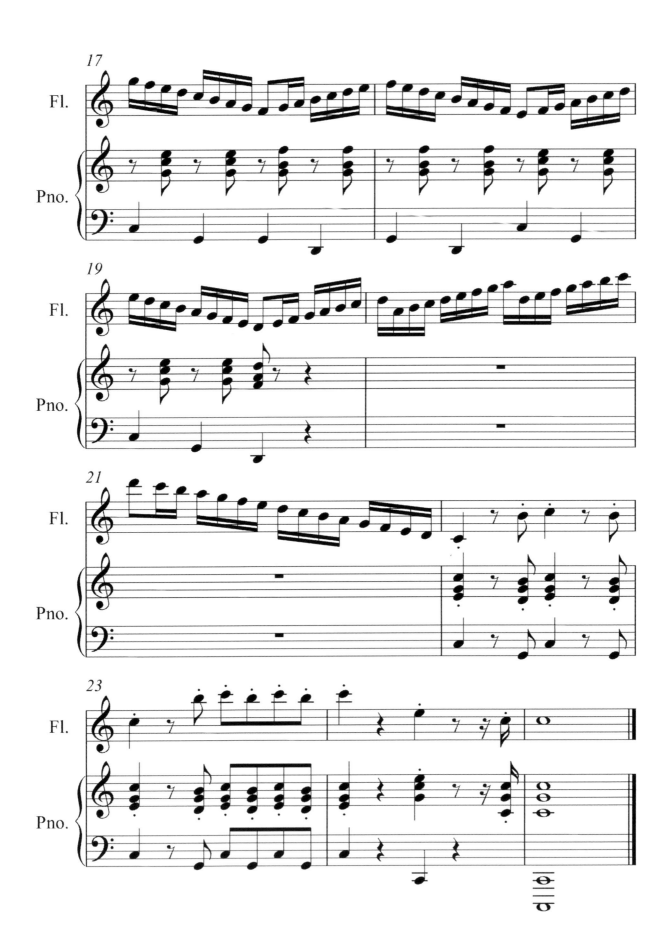

About the Author

Mike works as a professional musician and keyboard music teacher. Mike has been teaching piano, electronic keyboard and electric organ for over thirty years and as a keyboard player worked in many night clubs and entertainment venues.

Mike has also branched out in to composing music and has written and recorded many new royalty free tracks which are used worldwide in TV, film and internet media applications. Mike is also proud of the fact that many of his students have gone on to be musicians, composers and teachers in their own right.

You can connect with Mike at:

Facebook
facebook.com/keyboardsheetmusic

Soundcloud
soundcloud.com/audiomichaeld

YouTube
youtube.com/user/pianolessonsguru

I hope this book has helped you with your music, if you have received value from it in any way, then I'd like to ask you for a favour: would you be kind enough to leave a review for this book on Amazon? It'd be greatly appreciated!

Thank You
Michael Shaw

49315793R00032

Made in the USA
Lexington, KY
01 February 2016